A GATHERING OF PRAISE

Eden Press

A GATHERING OF PRAISE

Edited by
Rebecca Mee

First published in Great Britain in 1999 by Poetry Today, an imprint of
Penhaligon Page Ltd, 12 Godric Square, Maxwell Road, Peterborough. PE2 7JJ

A Catalogue record for this book is available from the British Library

ISBN 1 86226 577 1

Typesetting and layout, Penhaligon Page Ltd, England
Printed and bound by Forward Press Ltd, England

Foreword

A Gathering Of Praise is a compilation of poetry, featuring some of our finest poets. The book gives an insight into the essence of modern living and deals with the reality of life today. We think we have created an anthology with a universal appeal.

There are many technical aspects to the writing of poetry and *A Gathering Of Praise* contains free verse and examples of more structured work from a wealth of talented poets.

Poetry is a coat of many colours. Today's poets write in a limitless array of styles: traditional rhyming poetry is as alive and kicking today as modern free-verse. Language ranges from easily accessible to intricate and elusive.

Poems have a lot to offer in our fast-paced 'instant' world. Reading poems gives us an opportunity to sit back and explore ourselves and the world around us.

Contents

Prayer And Thanksgiving

We thank you Lord,
For all is safely,
Gathered in.
Merry sounds,
Of haymakers,
Have long faded.
With winter's
Light footfall.
Birds migrate, from
Hearth of home,
Harvest city bereft,
Only lone sentinel
Watches, and waits.
Lord, allow us
Not to become
Too complacent,
Lest we forget,
The needy,
Who only,
See mirage banquets,
As we give thanks,
To you,
Oh Lord,
Let us pray,
They will n'er,
Go hungry,
This night.

Terri Fisher

Thanks To God's Almighty Hand

Bringing home the harvest, the farm workers sweat and toil,
as they did in springtime, ploughing and preparing the soil,
once the land was ready, a wide variety of seeds were sown
which had to be looked after, until all those crops had grown.

In bygone days 'twas man and horse, their tools were rather stark,
and work was done in daylight, nothing ever ventured after dark,
the horse was stabled up each night, after a good brush and feed,
man and horse where in unison, as they went about their daily deed.

This modern day is so different, 'High Tec' machinery is at hand,
and a common sight to see tractors, after dark, working the land,
technology has taken over, hedges and dykes have disappeared,
causing a loss of wild life, something nature lovers always feared.

The summer season produces sights, like fields of golden wheat,
carrots onions and potatoes, and many other crops for us to eat,
the farmer take a big gamble, when he sows seed in the field,
for he has to rely on the weather, to ensure the crops will yield.

Once the crops are gathered in, we then give thanks to the Lord,
adorning the church with our harvest, and all sing with great accord
in our prayers we speak of many things, like God's almighty hand,
allowing us to plough the fields, and scatter seeds upon the land.

Wenn - The - Penn

Gather It In

Pick the olives and make the oil,
gather the grapes before they spoil,
crush them, press them to heady wine;
harvest the corn while the weather's fine,
then grind it down to make the bread;
but man needs more than bread it's said,
so turn the grass to make the hay,
put straw in the barn for a winter's day,
tend the cows, the hens and the sheep,
for milk and eggs and wool to keep
us warm and snug.

Reap the golden, pungent rape,
don't let the blue linseed escape
the crushing wheels that squeeze the juice;
cut flowers for decorative use,
trim back the bushes, clear the path,
chop logs to burn in the roaring hearth;
collect the apple, cherry and pear,
gather the ripening harvest fare;
fill the barn, the larder and store,
give thanks to God for this and more
on every day.

Wendy Ray

Shadows Of The Cross

Three shadows cast upon the wall
By the cross of Jesus dangling on a rope -
Shadows prompting past recall
Of the Church, charity, faith and hope.

The shadow of struggle in my youth
For sustenance of body and soul,
Searching always for the truth,
Knowledge, wisdom and self-control.

The ceiling elaborately painted with Angels
Was beautiful and awesome to behold -
Jesus, His Mother Mary, and Joseph,
His birth, his life and love retold.

A visit later with my young daughter,
A curious and beautiful child
Who looked up and said 'Mother,
Are we in Heaven?' She was beguiled.

The art work has since been replaced
By wooden beams and paint plain white,
The cross hangs now in the centre,
Three shadows cast by window light.

The second shadow is the present,
Carrying His cross of pain each day
Intermingled with the joy of living,
Joining our Saviour along the way.

The third shadow is the future
Which could be long or brief -
Will we join Him in Heaven
Just as he promised the thief?

The Church's interior decor has changed
But the exterior remains the same,
All lives to be enriched and rearranged -
Those shadows to follow again.

Floriana F Hall

Shimviveller 11
(The tale of a Combine Harvester)

Cottages stood empty and fell unrepaired
Farmers were now bountiful they did not flinch or care
As their trusted labourers faded from the scene
The land that once produced a thousand fold was reverting to fields of green
Eventually that great machine almost expired
But was resuscitated and thoroughly overhauled
As it changed the lifestyles and ways throughout many a workers home
Those farmers depended upon it as part of the farmyard equipment so inspired

What of those lads now unemployed many fell fail as their earnings lacked
With very little pittance some received opened a co-operative farmers bank
They then purchase produce like those before a more modern version of course
What is more unlike many others this machine is remote control
and can face any weather this was their resource

This harvester was programmed to guide
Requiring no operator from its tiny cabin
To the fields this mechanical wonder was put to work and surprise of surprise what has happened
Both day and night for its duty it has never shirked
'Shimviveller' you are a credit and an invention so fine
You saved many human beings from the dole queue line
It seems so uncanny in a field of golden shimmering wheat
A harvesting mechanic alone is reaping there is no human being on the seat

R D Hiscoke

Hands - A Grace

O Father God, for heavenly hands stretched out
in gracious love and care towards us,
we give you thanks.

For hands, O Lord, of those who sowed the seed,
and held the tractor's wheel and harvested the grain,
we give you thanks.

For hands, dear Lord, of honest traders, workers, rich
and poor, who brought, sold and carried far these foods,
we give you thanks.

For loving hands, our Lord, of those who long prepared,
cooked and presented this your plenty for us,
we give you thanks.

For able hands, good Lord, and bodies fit and strong,
to reach out and eat, enjoy and digest,
we give you thanks.

For your hands, O Christ, stretched out in love and
anguish for our souls on Calvary's tree,
we praise, and give you thanks!

Amen

Andrew G Phillips

One Time

One time I was a land girl
I rose reluctantly each morn
But the rising was less irksome
When there were poppies in the corn

Girls from Muston Hostel
Dawn 'till dusk they bent their backs
Spud picking behind the spinner
Then into potato clamps or sacks

Came sugarbeet lifting time
Hands stained black by leathery leaves
Forked into trucks behind the tractor
The will of heart moved aching arms and knees

Winter was hedging and ditching
Wellied feet into icy water you'd plunge
Flush away ragged hedges above you
In the ditch shovel out the gunge

But best of all I loved the harvest time
Reaping, stroking, feeling, seeing ripened corn
Studded with startling crimson poppies
An amazing picture every morn.

Barbara Robson

Harvest Time

Effervescent haze
Denotes autumn's gaze
Nature's bounty
Found in every county
The cornstalks stand like footsoldiers
In the field
A testament to God's goodness
And nature's yield
Each apple that falls
Signifies God's call
To the child of the wind
That His Son has smiled
On each drop of fruit
It's overwhelming goodness does shoot
A new reminder of harvest rays
Anxious for heavenly days
The reward for the man that prays.

Finnan Boyle

Harvest Hymn

Father God, we look around us
At this lovely world You made,
All the myriad scents and colours,
For Your glory all displayed!
Thank You for Your rich provision,
Meeting every creature's need,
Cold and warmth, and rain and sunshine,
Life within each tiny seed.

Father God, we are so thankful
That You give our daily bread,
That, again, our land is fruitful,
Harvest comes, just as You said;
Help us share Your gracious bounty
With each person who has need,
For You teach us in the Bible
We must love in word and deed.

Father God, as we, Your children
Praise and worship You today,
We're so thankful for this harvest
But we also want to say . . .
Thank You, thank You, Heavenly Father,
That You gave Your only Son,
That He died alone on Calvary,
And has our salvation won.

Mary Weeks

Excuse Once A Year To Thank God

I don't really know what harvest is
It sounds to me like a Holy event
When people emphasise their love and appreciation
Of the world through praying,
And share food together.
It sounds like an excuse once a year to thank God,
But one can make it be harvest everyday,
A season that lasts all year round.

Jahanara Khatun (16)

Dear Father God

Thank you for our daily bread.
A heavy responsibility lies upon your head.
Thou art the giver of all life's needs.
And from your abundance of wealth and
Overwhelming generosity we feed.
The patient farmer laboriously sows his seeds.
And prays a good harvest the rich soil yields.
But only by the power and love of God divine.
Does the refreshing rain fall and the glorious sun shine.
The dancing shimmering grain gilds golden bright,
And softly quivers with spontaneous pleasure and
sheer delight.
God's love whispers, gently rippling through the fields of wheat.
And they lay their hearts contentedly at His feet.
God of the pastures, meadows and fields you leave us
totally mystified.
As we view the harvest with awesome wonder, joy and pride.
We lift our voice in praise and adoration
And thank you for your loyal devotion.
You leave us feeling humble in your sight
God of love power strength and might.
The harvest moon looms big, orange and bright.
and accompanies the farmers in the still evening light.
The giant combine harvester very soon strips the field bare.
And for the birds who found shelter I have a care
And please harvest mouse make quick your escape.
For I fear the life of you and your family is at stake.
Once the store sheds and hoppers are filled to the brim
And the straw finally baled and safely gathered in
Only then is the harvest feast and merry making ready to begin.
At the harvest festival Hymns of thanksgiving joyfully ring
Praising God our heavenly Father, provider, Saviour and King.
Proudly is displayed God's harvest of love, from the crops
Of potatoes, fruit, and vegetables. All grown to grace the table, fit
for a King.

Again we thank the Lord for He is kind, and restores peace of mind

Help us dear Father God to scatter seeds of goodwill,
love and hope.
So we may help others less fortunate to cope.
For a bumper harvest we must pray.
To take the burden of sorrow, loneliness and
pain away.

Elizabeth Crellin

For Each . . .

For each leaf that's produced
that we consume,
let us not once overlook,
the best that we should employ each day
is taken from your book.

For each seed we plant
to fill the fields
and eagerly transport,
may the one that germinates the most
be the tiny seed of thought.

For each root we dig
from nourished earth,
for each fruit and daily bread,
we give grateful thanks that with your help,
the roots remain widespread.

In our need to sustain and grow,
may we continue to reap what we sow.

Diane Lack

Picnic

Resting in shimmering silverspoons,
Under white-sailed, summer blue,
Satisfied by ripe, sun-warmed peaches,
And chunk of sharp, country cheese,
New-made bread and drowsy wine.
Lulled into a false sense of time,
By the feast and fruited potion,
Accompanied by music of the day,
Where the river's gentle lapping,
Joins the bass hummed by bees,
Lovesick crickets add percussion,
While the skylark's crystal notes
Fall from the suspended arch of time.
Weighting eyes that will not open,
Though they see the shaded sun,
Glowing orange, through dropped lids.
As the mystic music lingers on,
Bewitching with a binding spell,
That I, cosseted by warm air,
Perfumed by the scent of earth,
Have no power, or desire, to resist
And I am content simply to exist.

J K Wood

A Grace

I am grateful Lord from breakfast to supper
I thank you for each cheering cuppa
For each morsel that graces my lips
Of bread and fruit and dear Lord, chips
Always we have enough to eat
Be it savoury, be it sweet
In our world I know others do not
In this grace I give them thought
I remember the hungry in this prayer
Those for whom the cupboard is bare
Nourish their spirit, enrich their souls
Let us work together to fill their bowls

Jeanette Latta

The Lord's Harvest

We're looking at the harvest Lord, amazed at what we see
The task is quite beyond us Lord, and so we turn to Thee.
The view is full of sadness, and so many souls are lost.
They're ignorant in the darkness Lord of what salvation cost.
They do not know of Jesus, they are groping in the dark
They are blind to all the suffering on that cruel cross so stark.

Our souls are full of yearning to tell them of His love
And how our hearts are burning with your spirit from above.
Help us heavenly father to shed your love abroad,
To tell them of your Kingdom and the message in your word.
By your precious Holy Spirit give us the power that we need,
For saving souls that now are lost, help us to sow the seed.

We're looking at the harvest Lord, so much to gather in
We're pleading now on their behalf to save them from their sin.
The labourers are few you said, so please accept our prayers
And even in our weakness Lord, as wheat to save those tares.
We're longing for the Harvest, white when it is gathered in
That no soul will be lost dear Lord in darkness black and grim.

Sybil Wesley

Lord Of The Harvest

As autumn leaves turn to flame,
It's time to till the fields again,
Prepare the earth, each year the same,
To plant the harvest fields with grain.

The seed lies dormant through winter days,
Under the frozen snow and earth,
Until the spring sun's warming rays,
Awakes the seed to birth.

Soon we see small green shoots,
Growing in the sun and rain,
Strengthening up their tiny roots,
To grow into perfect grain.

At last we see golden ears of corn,
Waving in the gentle breeze,
Soon reapers will these fields adorn,
And cut the corn with ease.

Our food is grown by God above,
For he provides the rain and sun,
He supplies our needs, with all his love,
For each and everyone.

Lord of the Harvest of earth and sea,
You're there to give whatever we need,
We offer our prayers of thanks to Thee,
And you give your love to all indeed.

Lord of all Harvests, you reap human souls,
And gently call them to your loving care,
As shepherd you place them in the folds,
Then take them above your home to share.

Violet Mary Swaine

Daily Provision

Open wide the windows and let the sunshine in,
Never wear a frowning face replace it with a grin,
You'll find your many blessings are too numerous to count,
Your obstacles and drawbacks will be easy to surmount.

Consider how the lilies grow, they do not
Spin nor do they sow,
Yet Solomon in all his glory could not outshine
These flowers of mine.

'Observe their beauty' Jesus said,
'They toil not for their daily bread,
Nor do they fret about tomorrow,
For each day gets its share of sorrow.'

He bids you ask for fresh supplies each day
For he knows your need,
New every morning rich bounty arrives
His whole creation to feed.

A banquet he spreads for man and beast
And bids all creation partake of the feast,
His ear is tuned into every sound,
He sees every sparrow that falls to the ground.

As long as the heavens and earth endure
He's ever faithful, ever sure
Come rain or sunshine, snow or hail,
Seed time and harvest shall never fail.

Mary G Kane

Harvest Givenness

Creation's givenness praise,
The sun's resplendent light;
Glad new-born life, brightest days,
The fair earth's fruitful might.
Love's sweet way, true faith inspires,
With the rainbow of peace.
Partnership meets deep desires,
Harvest-tide's prime showpiece.

Nature's stillness hides seed's growth,
Rich goodness shines in grain;
Unseen Creator keeps troth,
Sending refreshing rain.
Spring wakes from wintry gloom,
Meadows welcome bird-song;
In copses snowdrop clumps bloom,
Fruits ripen with élan.

Worldwide harvests' fullness yield,
From land and oceans deep;
The mineshaft and sunk oil-field,
Vast herds of cattle and sheep;
Are ours as trustees to share.
From neglect and wastage,
We help neighbours who despair,
Support souls in bondage.

Oneness is our destiny.
With the skills of science,
Bring hope to our progeny,
In a world alliance.
Thanks without deeds is blindness,
Uproot hate, sow goodwill;
Aid folk with loving-kindness,
Plenty for all fulfil.

James Leonard Clough

Harvest Days

Burnished gold the brown corn wavers . . .
Beneath the charm of harvest moon,
The season's yield soon to be gathered -
As summer plays her 'final' tunes.

Orchard boughs hang full and heavy . . .
Sheened and ripe the fruits now shine,
Glistening like red glowing rubies,
Jewels of the summer time.

All around green flowing meadows -
Tall grasses dance as changing tides,
Turn the 'patterns' of the season . . .
Far across the countrysides.

Malcolm Wilson Bucknall

September Song

This morning the windows breathed autumn mist,
condensed a white curtain on the dawn.
The city spires were sharpest lines,
etched on hydrangea clouds.
My fingertips tingled, and the dogs still shivered,
unsure if rowans, chestnuts on the grass
and crinkled sycamores could really mean
that Michaelmas is nearly here,
all blue and orange, speckled
petals for the big Archangel.

Janine Fitzpatrick

Harvest (My Old School)

Harvest meant to
Me as a boy
Take some food
To school.

Everyone did and
There was so much
I couldn't believe were
It all would go.

I thought we fat
Teacher will they eat
It all, all that food
Standing so told.

Only then I heard
The food was given too
People to poor too eat.

I felt so proud
That all my school
Had done so much,
I felt how many
Kind people there are.

E Sheldon

Whose Harvest Thanksgiving

Come ye thankful people come
Fills the church with a resounding ring
It's Harvest Festival, the organ plays
The congregation sing

Every nook and cranny
Is trimmed with fruit and veg
Beautiful flower arrangements
On every window ledge

Pillars festooned with flowers and corn
Loving hands have made the display
Surrounded by God's gratuitous gifts
Gaze in wonder at the array

All is safely gathered in
But not for us alone
A small church mouse surveys the scene
His harvest has come home

Poor as a church mouse is often said
But he does not feel poor today
Nice kind people have all brought food
He can now find time to play

For one or two short days now
His food is all to hand
No need to nibble the prayer book
Or the candle on the stand

He has a choice of lovely food
His small tummy full at last
I only hope he stays in his hole
Until the service is passed

He may be one of God's creatures
With a right to be here that's true
But I don't want to sing 'All good gifts around us'
Standing on my seat in the pew.

Peggy Hunter

Thoughts At Harvest

Through many years we've sung with zest of bringing in the sheaves,
But now we have no sheaves to bring, as combines race the fields.
We used to rake the stubble through for ears of fallen grain,
But now there is no gleaning done as flames race o'er the fields.

It is a way of life that's changed, as men machines are using
For work that once was done by men, who laboured in the fields.
Whatever method may be used, in lands around the globe,
''Tis still the Lord who gives the seed, it's impetus to grow.'

Whilst we have food within our homes and other people starve,
Help us, dear Lord, to look with care at everything we use,
Aware of all the wasteful things we carelessly have used.
Depriving others of the chance, to live as well as us.

Lord, show us how to utilise, the resources of this world,
That all men may thy goodness share, and see the rainbowed sky.
That greed and hatred may be gone and all may live in peace,
Aware that in the Son of Man, we all may live in love.

Sheila E Groom

Hooray For Harvest

Hear the combine harvester
Drone its familiar summer sound
Harvesting the corn, ready to be ground
Into the floor for our daily bread
Where a grateful nation's mouths
Open, ready to be fed

Feel the surge of energy
This massive machinery gives
As it glides around the field
Like a dragon's roar it lives,
The engine parts well oiled and running smooth
Harmony between man, technology, and all that's good

Watch the farmers working
Their muscles rippling strong and bold
As they transfer the grain to trailer
Pouring like liquid gold

Count the number of bales
Made up from fresh cut straw
To line the floor of cow sheds
A warm bed for the stabled horse

Praise the Lord Almighty
And thank Him sincerely
For giving us the bread of life
And this wonderful sight to see.

Sheila Margaret Parker

Untitled

The farmers and the farm hands
Work hard upon the land
Growing food for everyone
With God's helping hand
For he send them the rain
And also provides the sun
Now when it comes to harvest time
We go to church to say, 'Our Thanks'
For all that he's done
Taking with us some of the crops
There's food in plenty for all of us
That's been grown on his land
From the flour we make our bread
From the fruit we make the wine
And from our hearts we give
Love to all mankind
But without the help of God
There would be no harvest time!

Pauline Haggett

The Father's Harvest

The farmer gathers the harvest
The wheat and the corn from the field
The juicy sweet fruit from the garden
All earth has its treasures to yield

God sends the golden sunshine
The sweet gentle rain to the earth
The tender buds ripen and flourish
The world delights in new birth

The apples bloom in the orchard
The corn blows in the breeze
All things mature in due season
The berries and fruits on the trees

The fields are ablaze with His glory
These miracles come from His hand
Food to nourish the spirit
All part of His wonderful plan

We bring the first fruits for His blessing
Approaching His altar with prayer
We humbly give thanks for His bounty
With grace we acknowledge His care

Margaret S McAlpine

Get This Harvest In

Pray God we can get this harvest in
Because it looks like rain
So speed up that combine
To fill that corn store again.

Pray God we can get this harvest in
Because it is getting rather late
So don't let that tractor and cart
Even begin to hesitate.

Pray God we can get this harvest in
Just one more field to go
But it is beginning to spot with rain now
Yet it will stay dry I know.

Keith L Powell

Reflections

The mountains wept with waterfalls
Like great majestic tears
Around the glen the old stone walls
Have stood for many years,
The fierce rain lashed 'midst howling gale,
On cattle standing still
Through trees the sound of moaning wail
Brought wet and shivering chill;
Dark brooding clouds of indigo
Come menacingly near
To saturate the sodden ground
Year after endless year
Among these wild and rugged glens
My thoughts are deeply felt
It moves me to remember when,
Before my God I knelt.
I feel a sense come over me of life
And its perspective, solutions now
At last I see and I can be objective,
Those ageless mountains comfort me
The brooding clouds above,
In all this wilderness I see
A God of power and love.

Nancy Marriott

September, Then

The waving fields and sundown show
The passing glow yet caste on green rip'd fruit
The passing of a season
For the countryside then desolate
In black forked branch
And baron field, the darkening night
In poisoned sod and damp afterglow
In what has been held out of sight.

Not far from the harvest joys
The tethered kind make their response
What time now for the blood letting
Who knows the terror for them, free once?
And those yet wild in sea and air
Land too they know their pastures
In the breathless pause their captors
Know, before our greed an overture.

For all our sought the plate to fill
Now made rank, diseased
Or experimental in terror
Until our grossness eased.
For poisoned now the earth and air
The waters running wild
In this we seek our future now
The bounty yet higher piled.

Moderation is not enough
Pontification foolish
Each creature must know
It is our wish
That in their freedom too
We celebrate survival
And liberty to all that lives
A future to life all.

John Amsden

Harvest

Drink a pint of milk a day,
An apple a day keeps the doctor away,
Be sure to eat up all your greens,
I wonder what all this means.

Protein gives the meat to grow,
Starch and sugar energy to go,
Fats are energy in store,
Fibre cleans your insides more.

Calcium gives you teeth and bones,
Iron healthy blood, she drones,
Vitamin A gives healthy eyes,
Vitamin B makes your brain wise.

Vitamin C gives healthy skin,
Vitamin D lets calcium in,
If you eat cereals, eggs, fish, meat,
Fruit, milk, veg, you'll illness cheat.

Susan Mary Robertson

Harvest Song

We thank the Lord for Harvest
For waving corn and grain
The berries from the hedgerows
For sun and softening rain.
We thank Him for the people
Who work in fields so green,
On Harvester and combine,
A great sight to be seen.

We thank the Lord for Harvest
Which gives our daily bread.
That all the whole world over
His people may be fed.
We thank the Lord for Harvest
That at the end of time
Our souls will be the Harvest
Of His great love divine.

Eunice C Squire

Funny For Some

It's a funny old world;
Sometimes not of our choice.
Some ride on a donkey;
Others in a Rolls Royce.
One half of mankind goes to bed;
Too hungry to sleep.
What the other half wastes,
Would make the other half weep.
It's a funny old world;
But I can't join in the mirth.
When what's supposed to be good;
Is destroying the earth.

Windsor Hopkins

Harvest

The autumn sun
lies gentle in the sky.
The wind
cuts across the meadow.
A solitary bird
does fly.
The farmer pulls
his heavy plough,
and thanks the lord
above,
for the fortune
and the glory,
that is alone god's love.
The days are cutting in
on him,
the autumn of
his life,
he looks to home
his family,
crowned
by his lovely wife,
and once again
he prays to god,
his harvest all
about.

Siobhan O'Conchubhair

Autumn Evening

Evening and autumn; lingering, the sun
Warms the old walls and shines on spires and towers
Making earth perfect. Then, his great task done,
He leaves the world so long, dream-haunted hours;
And the grey city lit with fading gold;
To the wind stealing in from fields of flowers,
Their petals closing as the dew falls cold.

To quiet of her low river and slow streams,
The peace which deep within the evening dwells
'Till the soft bells ringing waken her from dreams
With music silver as in pale sea-shells
Struck by the rippling waves in still moonlight,
Clear as the song of sphere; 'till those far bells
Call through the starlit vastness of the night.

Call as in sadness for earth's age-old pain.
Too short the golden calm the evening brings.
Beauty is broken, drowned in days of rain;
The moon is dark eclipse. And yet there sings
A lone bird in a land left dim and grey,
Its song like love for all the frailest things,
And sweetest sorrow at the close of day.

O autumn of immortal mystery
Reflecting splendour ever vanishing;
Late flowers in pools and sundown on the sea;
You, fairer far than ever was the spring;
For all her cool, blue days; what secret lies
Within the glimmering brightness which you bring?
From what new, shining place beyond the skies?

You tell how colour fades away too soon,
The glory of your forest's golden light
And glowing red of a great harvest moon
Rising above the jagged mountain height;
That winter comes with wind and wild white snow
And bitter death o'erwhelms the loved in night:
But beauty is eternal where they go.

Diana Momber

Harvest At The Allotments

The allotment growers viewed their harvest with pride
Reverently laying vegetables side by side
Hoping this year they'd win a coveted prize
The reward for outstanding quality and size
Their minds went back to the worries they'd had
And even when they had felt quite sad
Like when vegetables remained too small
Or bolted to turn out scraggy and tall
Feeding marrow's to make them juicy and thick
Worrying in case they'd become victims of a vandal's stick
Assessing rivals progress when passing their plot
Thinking smug smiles meant they'd win a lot

Excitement rises here comes the men of power
To give their judgement in an hour
Did one of them have a nervous blink
Or was he giving a contestant the wink
Vegetables peered at and thoroughly prodded
In agreement the judges finally nodded
Heavens above two prizes I've won
Usually my achievements have been none
It's to do with the judges there's no doubt
This year they all know what they're talking about

J Atkinson

Harvest Delight

Yellow corn, barley ripe
Old gardener, smoke from pipe
Apples rosy
Sweet posies
Nuts, all shining bright
Leaves dropping
Seeds still popping
In this season of delight.

Glorious colours
Earth all smothered
With the richness
Dropped from height
Nature caring
All preparing
For the sleeping
Of our Lord's delight.

Brenda Norman

Harvest Festival

The church is dressed in harvest gear;
  This time comes only once a year;
Ears of corn, wheat, barley and maize,
  Help to make this a day of days.

Harvest festival time again:
  There are even eggs from the hen;
Ladies with baskets of flowers;
  Oh, such busy, but happy hours!

Fruit and vegetables by the score,
  Even piled high behind the door.
All tended with such loving skill,
  Now the church is ready to fill.

Hands and backs have bended down low,
  To get this fine harvest to grow:
Now the toil and trouble is past,
  The harvest gathered in at last!

J Millington

Harvest

The bounteous earth gives up her sun-warmed green
And knee-deep meadows sigh on south-born air;
The wide-eyed daisy, innocent and free-
A fringe to field of symmetry and care.

The heavy bough, its sensuous perfume spent,
Sheds brown-edged flower in quiet humility,
The fruit unnoticed, bitter, hard: well hid
In leaves still raised in proud nobility.

And man responds to earth's primeval call;
Wields glinting scythe in unrelenting sway;
And does he pause to wonder whence it came?
This rich reward for labour's little day.

The once lush earth stands dead, her giving done,
But slowly dawns a bright, expectant morn,
And death is but the way by which man finds
The never-failing joy of faith reborn.

'While the earth lasts, seedtime and harvest, cold and heat, summer and winter, day and night, shall never cease.' Genesis: ch8 v 22

Eleanor Sames

Harvest

The bells ring out a joyous peal,
The song of harvest home is sung
While all around the gathered fruits are spread.

Within the porch two mighty marrows lie,
Flanked by beetroots, carrots, beans and apples red.
Around the font chrysanthemums in colourful display.

Each pew along the aisle a posy holds.
By the altar, a homemade cottage leaf,
Placed upon a leafy spray, garlanded by flowers.

I heard a voice beside me cry, 'Our crops lie waste,
The flooding waters rise and swamp the land'.
'Our years of patient toil are all in vain.'
The message plain for all to see.

You are blessed with plenty,
More than enough for all to share.
Spare a morsel, if you really care
For starving folk like me.

Noelle Wells

The Little Seed

A small bird dropped a seed of wheat within some soil.
In darkness it lay asleep,
a tiny heart beat.
Time passed and it stirred, began to swell,
to push and explore within its unlit cell.
A frail green shoot showed above the earth
that had given it sanctuary until its birth.
It looked about as it grew straight and tall,
and saw in the distance a city wall.
Its tiny, yellow ears of wheat slumbered in the noonday heat.
Then shouts and noise disturbed its calm.
A wooden cross like a mighty arm
was erected beside the plant in the sod,
bearing, outstretched, the Son of God.
The wheat, unmolested, grew at the Saviour's feet,
where, flecked with blood from His wounded head,
it dreamed of becoming Holy Bread.

Ellsie Russell

Harvest Time

Plough in the sun,
Reap in the rain,
Mix soil and seed into one,
And bring forth autumn again.

Lynda Cosgrove

Mongo Bendugu

(Dedicated to the people of Mongo Bendugu, a village in Sierra Leone, West Africa where I worked for two years.)

Rice is our staple diet
But where is the rice?
The ground is eroded
So where is the rice?

The ground is so poor
So where is the rice?
Tobacco was grown here
So where is the rice?

Cash crops were grown
So where is the rice?
The people were cheated
So where is the rice?

The sun is so strong
So where is the rice?
We have no rain
So where is the rice?

Children are hungry
So where is the rice?
They are malnourished
So where is the rice?

Women are weeping
So where is the rice?
The men are drinking
So where is the rice?

We are praying rain Lord
So where is the rice?
We trust in your care Lord
So where is the rice?

Our neighbours have given us
Some bags of rice
We cannot transport it
So where is the rice?

Many rats have been seen
So where is the rice?
Sold on the Black Market
So where is the rice?

The rains have come now
So where is the rice?
It is growing strongly
This wonderful rice.

Christine Webster

Fruit Harvest Time - Thank God

Up and down the ladders,
moving from tree to tree -
now, now - mind how you go -
'tell us . . . is it time yet for tea?'

It is the time for harvest,
whether apple, plum or pear -
no matter where one might wander -
one will find some solace there.

With ladder, clicks, and buckets -
such a hive of industry -
although 'tis but a few weeks work -
'twill fill one's heart with glee.

Some trees they'd be twisty -
and some'd be high and big -
yet one will surely manage,
whilst depending on that single twig.

Gladstone, Beauty of Bath -
Bramley Seedling, Grenadier -
Victoria, Damson, Cinnamon -
Thank God! - Harvest time is here.

Kevin McCann

A Season Well Spent

Rich scarlet berries growing on vines
drying in golden sun.
Yeald crimson vintage wines
we drink to fortune and good times,
the taste of raisin and ripe plum.

Earth's produce singing God's praises
celebration food, country kitchen fare.
On the stove, carrot and celery braises
jolly farmer a cup cider raises,
To his broody wifes, camomile washed hair.

Celebrates the coming birth; wild his leaping
shows his love, among the butter churns.
Grateful now the grain is gathered in
giving thanks to God and peace within,
sweet incense from fields of straw'burns.

Captures the essence of ancient rite's read
happy farmers gather at the mill.
Prayers of lavender and rosemary, loudly said
sprinkle with rose petals, the newly wed,
merry with cider, all have had their fill.

Sunday morning prayers and psalms
a child dressed as nature; wears a paper crown.
Weaves a potent spell of golden charms
fruits and flowers in her arms,
shakes the blossom from autumn's gown.

Seasons in the sun; scorching purple heather
yearling fields-purple cherry's-juicy pear.
Celebrated in fruits of the loom
there bright colour and perfume,
the song of harvest festival, everywhere.

Invoke, younger days of school bells ringing
brown sandals, wading through the leaves.
Our childish voices singing
we shall go rejoicing,
bring in the sheaves.

Jane Mary Evans

Thanksgiving

How I loved that autumn time -
When as a chorister of eight,
I sang with gusto tunes sublime,
The Harvest Home to celebrate.

All Country folk at Rogation,
Asked the Lord to bless the sowing;
That the larders of the Nation,
Might be filled to overflowing.

And then we gave to Him our thanks,
For rain and sunshine, wind and snow;
And congregations of all ranks,
Now praised His bounty here below.

Some had toiled the Church to brighten,
While others brought their gifts in kind;
Then when thoughts began to lighten,
All had gratitude in mind.

On the Chancel fruits and flowers,
Together with scrubbed veg, displayed;
Arrangements must have taken hours,
With all the flowers there arrayed.

New bread, fresh-baked like sheaves of wheat -
Were on the Altar gently laid;
And real sheaves tied up so neat,
The pew-end decoration made.

Sweet-smelling fruit on ev'ry ledge,
Around the pulpit and the font;
Along the sanctuary edge -
The posies that the children want.

At the end they queue with others,
And hold the little gifts above;
As they dash back to their mothers,
To whom they give them with their love.

A O Jones

Harvest Time

What's different about our school today?
Where's the smell of blackboards, books and bodies?
No it's fruit and veg and tins, I say,
All given to make parcels of goodies.

In the hall, the tables are all set up,
Apples, oranges, pears, bananas and cherries;
Potatoes, turnips, carrots and sprouts,
And from mum's deep freeze-even berries.

Little people stagger in, their arms so full,
With boxes and bags and sacks,
Walking up to the tables so calm and cool,
Enthusiasm-not one child lacks.

At eleven o'clock everyone there,
Grandparents especially invited,
The vicar arrives and blesses the 'fare'
The children are so excited.

The words of the hymns really matter,
To everyone in the room you see,
'We plough the fields and scatter'
And 'Those in peril on the sea'

The service ends - fruit and veg collected,
Happy Grandparents leave the school,
Hurrying home-produce carefully selected,
Everyone content and happy - that's the rule..

Whatever is left is handled with care,
And children set off to deliver,
To the people who couldn't come this year,
For one reason or another.

Dorothy Whitehall

Dewdrops

I glimpse a thousand dewdrops in a field
Amidst quiet meadows burgeoning with grass -
A thousand dewdrops glistening like gems,
Whose mirror image gleans rich harvest's yield
Of eastern sunrise as soft zephyrs pass
Among a host of gently shimmering stems.

Each one a diamond in its own right,
Unique in colour, shape and lustrous tint;
A snowflake out of season, out of time;
Each one a still reminder of the night,
Inflamed anew by dawn's awakening glint
As myriad ears of corn reach their prime.

And yet, how soon each bead of dew dissolves
In just a wink as sunbeams warm cold ground.
How soon each brittle jewel - each vaporous drop -
Blinks a last goodbye, and then resolves
Into fine elements without a sound.
Where is now the harvest? Where the crop?

Rainbows of delight upon each hedgerow,
Diamond-hard, it seems; and yet, how soft
As all that gossamer of precious stones,
Evaporating, melts with fading glow
From every meadow, country field and croft,
Extinguishing those cloying dewdrop clones.

How transient we human beings are,
Just like those lambent droplets. Here today
And gone tomorrow, we are rainbow hues
More volatile than any shining star
Whose cosmic diamond-studded overlay
Combines with crystal whites and sapphire blues.

And yet, how precious, cherished and unique
Each of us is to Christ, our Risen Lord,
Whose living word formed dewdrops of Creation
From chaos, and whose Hands, mild and meek,
Were torn by violence, strife and disaccord,
That we might reap rich harvests of elation.

Robert D Hayward

The Gift Of Bread

The swaying cornfields gleam beneath the sun,
Not flattened by assaults of wind or rain,
For wise plant-breeders such results have won
That we shall reap a richer crop of grain.

In olden days a village was sustained
With work for many in the harvest fields.
Such usages have clearly not remained -
Few needed now to bring in larger yields.

(But should machines come under an attack?
To earn a living there are other ways:
The old-time worker with his breaking back
May operate computer-screens these days).

The husky grains are processed into flour
And pass along to test the baker's art:
And then imagination shows its power
As many shapes and colours play their part.

For simple spheres and rectangles do not
Exhaust the baker's notion of a shape,
For plaited, squat or drawn-out forms we spot
Across the world's wide dietary landscape.

In third-world countries they are less concerned
With fantasy of shape to please the eye:
Produced in their own ovens, they have learned
Their families' needs themselves to satisfy.

In all our varied cultures we must praise
The God who gave us all the means to live;
With love we, too, should try to find the ways
To seek out others' needs, to share, to give.

And Christ is our example: He refused
To turn the stones to bread when just for show,
But multiplied the loaves when they were used
To feed the hungry crowds with hearts aglow.

And earthly bread He really sanctified
When He made it His body, gift of love:
In holy mystery we're unified
With one another and with God above.

For earthly and for heavenly food, O Lord,
For helping soul and body both to grow,
Your people give You thanks with one accord
Whom one day we may still more closely know.

Anne Sanderson

How Lucky We Are

If we are hungry, there's food in our homes,
There are shops nearby.
We can satisfy our hunger
For a pound or two.
Thank God for giving us food.

Unlike our far-off neighbours
In dry, desert places
Where nothing grows
And the ground cracks for thirst,
We do not have to fear hunger.
Thank God for giving us food.

We have enough to share
And feed our families
So we may sleep at night.
Our dreams are of other desires;
Faces flushed with health.
Thank God for giving us food.

V E Forester

Apple Flattercakes

Eager to multiply the moments
of our seaside holiday
we crept out when the seagulls called
raced half a mile to morning Mass.
Tangy smell of lemon, apple
mingled with the chime of bells
hastily we splashed our foreheads
ran across the Tenby road.

Ducking under the Five Arches
we dodged the milkman's horse-drawn cart
oven-warm the cake shop beckoned
cream cakes, jam tarts, crusty bread
smiled invitingly at us
five small children morning hungry
green eyes darting, laughter gurgling
jostling, reaching, hands outstretched

I want this one oozing honey,
no, the one with sugar's best,
or that one full of sticky cherries,
Tim chose 'apple flattercakes'.
What Tim said always won the day
it was the serious way he said it
made us feel unless we followed
we'd miss the one important thing.

We dawdled down the cobbled street
clomping with our sandalled feet
five pairs of green eyes kept returning
to the bag in Timmy's hands.
Let's go back along the seafront
watch the waves crash on the rocks
there's plenty time before our breakfast
we might just try one flattercake.

Mum, in blue, was at the door
where have you been and did you get
the breakfast bread, and why're your fingers
all so sticky? Is that sugar on your chin?
Tim looked up with wide surprise
all innocent and cherub faced:
'We came back by the promenade
the waves whooshed up their salty spray.'

Oonagh Twoney

Lammas

Gold gasps its last,
leaks red
where the sun's grain goes
below
earth's brow and breast
shorn short
to harvest heaven's
gold glow.

Chris Moat

I Am What I Am

I am what I am said I
And no one will ever change me
I'll walk with no care for anyone
So what do I care if I hurt you.
Walked on 'till I tired
Then sat on a log
To the bees and the birds
I did listen
Hummed and chirped
In a sweet genial air
Seemly cheering me up
Sure I love you, just as you are,
Without any doubt
Filled me up with such love
I recall now the words that I heard
Be loving and gentle
Just like the Lord
Leaving a trail of love
For all to follow
Put everyone of your hopes.
In this flower of love
To nourish all of your tomorrow's
My love.

Margaret Mary Hurley

Starved

The poor say thank you for a crust of bread,
And for somewhere to lay their head.
The sun is hot and burns all day,
I wish I had a drink they say.
The sun's so hot and won't go away,
We're so exhausted we can't even play.
The flies keep biting our tiny heads,
They circled round us, at least they're fed.
Where will we get a bite to eat,
In this dreadful heat.
The night time comes and cool it gets,
No clothes to wear so cold it is.
The illness pays its toll at night,
And takes away the will to fight.
Those who die escape too quick,
But we're all left, who takes the pick.

Heather Ann Breadnam

Rowan Harvest

The Scottish scene,
Observed of human eyes -
All heather-wreathed and rugged,
Mist-drenched and loch-spattered,
Invites a bird's-eye view.
        And more than view;
        For here is sustenance,
        The glowing fruits in bunches,
        Aching with juice and vitamins,
        Providing nourishment.
Blackbird and thrush
Come early to the feast,
Greedily devouring unripe berries -
The reddening remainder seized upon
Be redwing and fieldfare.
        All these soft bills,
        Enjoying succulence,
        Evacuated the hard seeds,
        Splurged on the ground
        Where they had fed.
Greenfinches, other-mannered,
Perch and peck with dextrous beak
To rid the precious seed
Of its encumbering flesh
Discarded like litter after a picnic.

Garth Waite

Thanksgiving

During my younger days
I watched her each Sunday
Immaculately dressed she walked
With umbrella in hand
Navy coat hat and matching gloves
Smartly she went to church.

In early autumn we were treated to the visit -
She always took us to see the display
Prepared lovingly by the congregation for harvest thanks.
As the door creaked upon, the sunlight poured in
Through arched windows casting a hazy mist over the pews.
It was so silent - awaiting the exultation to come.

Flowers arranged perfumed the air, vegetables scrubbed
Sheaves of golden wheat and corn
Contrasted with apples red and green
Spoils to be divided among the poor after praise
A truly Christian thing to do
To thank God for his goodness all year through.

Sarah A P Gallagher

Harvest Home

Through the open kitchen window in the tender light of dawn
Farmer, eager, views his fields of amber grain
The swelling heads, in unison, are waving their good morn'
As the farmer thanks his Lord for sun and rain.

Though his weathered hands are callused and his body yearns for rest
Farmer, knowing, sees the day at last has come
To call upon the strength and fortitude with which he has been blessed
And 'tween dawn and dusk to bring his harvest home.

From the orange-tipped horizon where the grain had kissed the skies
Farmer, weary, views his fields of golden sheaves
Another harvest safely gathered as the summer says goodbye
And the autumn says 'hello' with falling leaves.

Kath Wiles

The Old Wicker Basket

The old wicker basket stood in the hall,
For years it was Grandmother's friend.
Always on her arm when she came round to call,
Its life seemed to have no end.

For the children there would be an apple or sweet
From the depths of the basket, or some kind of treat.
While to the sick and the lonely then you may depend,
The sight of that basket meant 'here comes a friend'.

As spring turned to summer and harvest time yields,
The basket carried fourses to the men in the field.
Wiping the sweat from their brows would laugh,
Swigging tea from a bottle, scones fresh from the hearth.

Cold winter nights when the wild wind was moaning,
The basket was full of Grandpa's wool stockings.
Chestnuts or onions would roast in the embers,
As Grandma darned stockings and told of days she remembered.

Then Grandma died, and the sadness did fall,
The basket stood empty pushed back in the hall.
All covered with dust, just ordinary, humble,
But I couldn't give grandmother's basket for jumble.

So once more the basket will serve the living,
Filled with vegs and fruit at the Harvest Thanksgiving
On the font in the church when Grandma was wed,
For what is given with love can never be dead.

G M King

Supermarket Praise

Wandering round the supermarket aisles
I reminisced, remembering
My country parish church and
The annual Harvest Festival -
The decorated loaves and
The sheaves of corn around the altar.
The usually drab window ledges
Adorned with colourful fruit
And flower arrangements by
The ladies of the parish;
The choir and congregation singing
Lustily, 'We plough the fields and scatter'
And, 'Come ye thankful people, come'.

So why don't we

Strip all these well-ordered shelves,
Stack the glowing fruit and veg,
The bottles of wine, French sticks and do'nuts
And have an urban Harvest Celebration?
The store manager could invite in all and sundry
To eat, drink and be merry
And sing together the Harvest songs.
Then all the cheerful, contented folk
(Including the manager) could go away
Happy in the knowledge that
For a short time at least
They had become the 'thankful people'
Of the hymn in remembering the Donor
Of so many 'good gifts around us'
That find their way on to the
Supermarket shelves.

Maria-Christina

The Plougher

On the up land field I see
The plough man at work once more
Seems but yesterday
Since he gleaned its harvest store

How faithfully he does his work
He labours his very best
To make the ground fit for the seed
He know God will do the rest

So the seasons roll along
Obeying his divine command
Winter's snow and spring's warm sun
To mature our own dear land

The fulfilment of his plan goes on
Although we have storms and gales
Although we murmur and fret
Seed time and harvest never falls

Stella Brown

An Abundance

A myriad of activity abounds as mother, father and Aunt Sally
rally to gather the crops,
Some for sale, some for ourselves, some for the church -
an abundance - all gathered in our laps;
Large greengages, green and purple grapes all planted and watered
by father's magical hands,
The wagon groans under their tremendous weight - a few, new
welcome ones this year grown from seeds brought back
from foreign lands.

The smell of freshly picked fruits and cut flowers fills me with
joy,
They'll soon be eaten by us all-man, woman, girl and boy;
I marvel at these luscious foods provided for us to eat
I long for God to explain the secret of His creations while
sitting at His Royal feet,

'How did He achieve the many, varied tastes and species?'
This I ask myself as we pluck them from their branches -
apples, berries, cherries and peaches.
I gather them into my sinewy arms and place them in large
welcoming bags -
I am dressed for the part-not in a smart suit but in my
everyday rags.

The harvest is a plenty, every mouth has been fed,
We are all fulfilled, watered and ready for bed;
There is much more for us - we shall put the rest in store
And we now kneel by our beds and give thanks to the
Good Lord - He whom we honour and adore.

Margaret Andrews

Corn Have Got Ears

Cornfields of all yellow and tan,
Ears of corn growing across fields and lands -
You have to walk quiet through the corn in sun,
For the ears of the corn will trap you for fun -
Wheat of harvest or corn flakes on a plate,
Beware how you crunch them of the noise that you make.
Lovers of lust in cornfields lay,
Must be aware that the farmer comes not their way -
At night the ears of all cornfields are at rest
In sweet dreams - they sway -
That is why no one yet knows how the corn circles are made.
Wake up all you ears of corn at night.
Then you can tell us all about the big circles bright -
O ears of corn do please stand on your guard when harvest
Time comes along
Listen for the harvester with its cutting blades,
The ears of corn close their eyes and ears - in hope
It goes away -
Now so sad for the corn have been all cut,
No more will the ears of corn hear
And their eyes will forever stay shut -
Flattened now are the fields, all corn reaped
And bundled tight,
Soon this year's ears of corn will be gone forever
From our sight -
O what a nasty shame
But next year - new corn with ears will
Grow in fields once more again -

Marion Staddon

Harvest Song

Fiery glory of an autumn daybreak
Bursts across the radiant sky,
Trees aflame with blazing colour,
Hips and haws and orange berries,
Cones and acorns falling fast,
Birds and squirrels busy searching -
Harvest morning.

Corn is cut and stooked and gathered,
Swifts are circling overhead
Catching insects on the wing,
Bats and moths and owls appearing,
Dusk begins to turn the sky
Glowing into gold and green.
Harvest twilight.

E D Sulston

Contemplation Beneath A Tree In Autumn

Old, silent and still,
With the wisdom of years.
No worries, no cares,
Ravaged by storms
But anchored to earth
By a tangle of roots.

How weathered your bark
Like an old piece of leather.
Your myriad branches stretch to the sky.
Countless leaves turning
Brown, rust and yellow
Fall to the ground. Lie,
No longer needed.
Dead.

Oh, what could you teach me, my tree,
About patience?
About firmness of purpose
And frail human need?
How storms of life pass,
And every spring is preceded
By the mists of autumn
And winter's cruel face?

What is it I see when I note your stillness?
Is it indifference?
Surrender? Decay?
Oh, no, my noble friend
It is surely tranquillity,
Serenity, composure,
And the triumphs of age.

Teach me, my tree,
How to gain your detachment,
How to submit with resignation,
To acquiesce, or bend if need.
How accomplishments count for nothing
And the victor's laurel wreath
Is composed of leaves
Already dying.

That living with a single purpose
Reaching upward every day, with roots
Firmly embedded in what to others
May appear clay,
Is the one and only aim in life
With which to be concerned.

For sharing this knowledge,
For experienced gained,
Thank you, my tree, my friend.

Marie Hopkinson

Harvest At School

When I was at school
I do recall,
of gathering together
in the main hall.
Chattering and shuffling
sat legs crossed,
cold in our behinds
and hymn books embossed.

We'd sing of golden fields
at harvest time,
ripe with all that maize.
Waiting for the farmer's hand,
in those harvest days.

The headmaster spoke of
woodsmoke air,
that's carried in the breeze.
And all the autumn coloured leaves
are falling from the trees.

But my favourite memories
where to see their faces
light up with such glee.
When boxes of beans, lentils,
tins of soup,
where taken to the old,
from all of us in class three.

Yvonne Tyerman

Harvest

When reapers view the golden land
  So full of promise and their just award,
And see the outcome of God's hand,
  From seed to harvest as a rich reward.

Then leaps their hearts in grateful praise
  As they begin the joyous harvest yield
To garner as the summer days
  Still lengthen out for workers in the field.

As stubble whitens o'er the earth
  And birds come darting down to glean
Such wayside spills of ample worth
  While over all - a dazzling rainbow scene

And in the hedgerows berries red
  Against the russet leaves and cobalt skies
Outshine the summer's fountainhead
  Of fruits and seeds as daylight dies.

While in the strawy thatch the birds
  Twitter and flutter all the livelong day,
Against the lowing of the herds
  Grazing in pastures 'midst the new-mown hay.

Nestling behind the stony walls
  Built by strong hands in distant ancient times,
Sheep and their lambs with bleating calls
  Sound out across the faint and misty climes.

And in the village church the hymns
  Of harvest, sung with lusty thankful heart
At morn and when the daylight dims
  Outpouring praise in every part

Spirit of harvest, blest, divine,
  Gather the whole of nature in your sway,
Enter into this longing soul of mine
  And grant a blessing as I pray.

R T James

Goodbye To Summer

Chilling autumn winds do blow
fires have a warming glow,
leaves once green begin to fall.
Winter soon, will on us call.

Summer days and evenings light
no longer with us warm and bright.
A sadness creeps into the heart
as a season does depart.

Frost and snow upon the ground
footsteps pass without a sound,
Christmas carols will be sung
icicles from windows hung.

Feelings deep and full of mirth
all because of Jesus' birth.
Christmas day the world be stilled
with happiness and laughter filled.

Maureen Hughes

Harvest Year

Bid farewell to shades of summer
Greens replaced by hues of brown.
Warm breezes sway the golden cornfields
Pheasants scour the ground
Mushrooms in the morning mist - hedgerows glisten -
Dew-drop kissed.
Apples in scarlet jackets dressed -
Waiting for the cider press
Leaves are falling, dried and fragile - trees
Will soon be bare.
Bonfires burning,
Lazy spirals drift into the humid air.
Skylarks rise in early evening - shrill notes pierce
The mind in waves.
A eulogy to passing days into winter's cold white grave.
Harvest moon in all its splendour
Rides the sky majestically.
Veils of shadows vie with moonlight -
Owls hoot plaintively.
Now the sounds of throbbing engines surge
Across the fields.
Harvesting the grains of summer
And all the good earth yields
Across the country every church is crowned
With nature's gifts.
Voices sing in unison for everyone to hear
We all must thank our God above - who
Through His everlasting love
Gave us our Harvest Year.

Elsie Francis

The Grain Of Wheat

The grain of wheat must die
in bearing life,
that of her substance she may grow
a golden head.
A golden head
of infinite worth,
of humble birth,
so crushed and ground and broken,
and powdered into bread.

The grain of wheat shall live
in suffering death,
for in her substance she shall be
of the Godhead.
Of the Godhead,
infinite worth,
no more of earth,
but raised and blessed and sanctified
a Host in form of bread.

Mary McKeone

Back End Of The Year

The sun shines on the dying roses, ah sweet deja vu.
Memories of times gone and to come again,
Weak September sunlight, October wind and rain.
The smell of garden fires links across the years,
To times we now think had no cares.

We don't remember now the scratchy hands,
Only the harvest of rose-hips, on someone else's land.
Bittersweet transition, it seems to some,
From glorious summer days, to storms to come.
The stars shine softly now, not glittering bright,
As on some November night.

Gathering flocks of birds fill the sky, in herds,
Swirling storms upon the western ocean,
Soon will put the trees in violent motion.
Warm in the house, we breathe a silent sigh;
Those summer days, why did thy have to die?
Harvest is in, to see the winter through,
Apples, corn and root crops too.

Lawrence Grey

Down And Out

Before me you stand, unkempt, with no one to care.
Inspite your smelly, shabby clothes your dignity remains.
Regularly I hear you arrive quietly, knocking for attention
The house a quiet refuge in the unknownness of your life.
A welcoming smile, a plate of food. You ask for little.
What thoughts have you, sitting outside our lives?
Shuttered in the tiny porch space allocated to you.
I met you again tonight, soaked through from the rain
Your world in a carrier bag at your feet.
Yet you complained not, your smile friendly, welcoming your words.
Deep within me I judged you. Then I wondered why.
For who knows, one day I could be the one sitting there
Compassion then stirred, and your greeting was returned.
How valued you the moment as fleetingly our lives touched?
Interlude over, my journey continued. Wondering at the emptiness,
At your loneliness, at the prospect of a life devoid of love.
Is there no one who cares? No family? No friends?
What caused your plight? Where do you go?
Sadly you had gone when I returned, leaving nothing
Save an empty plate, a lasting impression, a memory,
Of you, a man with no place to lie down
One of the many faceless, nameless, homeless
Outcast by the insular society of today.

Teresa Booth

The Return

I strolled through the countryside on a peaceful summer's day,
And the farmers they were busy, in the fields, making hay.
The cows the cud were chewing, and the sheep gave their gentle bleat,
It was wonderful to feel again, the grass beneath my feet.
I walked down by the river, and heard the familiar sounds,
Of the water running, over stones, in leaps and bounds.
A sudden flash of silver as a fish darted away,
From a blue Kingfisher, as it dived to catch its prey.

The fields of golden buttercups, and cowslips, here, and there,
And the gentle breeze that carried their fragrance, on the air,
All these things brought memories of my younger days,
When I worked in the fields, in the summer, making hay.
Ploughing, sowing, reaping, and tiling the fertile land,
Strolling home at the end of the day, with tired feet, and blistered hand.

But one day I'll come back again, and this time I will stay,
No more to search for fortunes in the cities, far away.
For here I need no fortune, no need to pay a fee,
Because life's most precious things, are here, and they are free.

Johann K S Brangham-Tucker

Bounty Of The Earth

Walking to school clutching
A crumpled brown paper bag
Containing an apple, an
Orange and a banana

Why do some people bring
Packets of biscuits or
Tins or soup? Don't their
Mums know you can't harvest

Them? I suppose the poor
Are grateful for anything
We give them after we've
Said the prayers and sung the hymns

I like the hymns, they
Make me feel good
Inside. But best of all
I like the smells

The smells of the
Fruit. And the great big
Giant Harvest loaf

You need to be rich
To buy one of those

Christine Walker Burns

Mr Moon

Mr Moon
grinds the wheat and corn
from early morn
barley mown
sails go round

Great cog wheels crush
the grains and husk
whilst Mrs Moon of ancient hour
bags by hand
the rough hewn flour

John Kirkham

Sounds Of Harvest

The tractor harvests mown grass
as silage for the cattle's feed
and while the work goes on apace
the vibrant engine drone
continues up and down the land.
At length the field is shorn of
grass
and tractor travels on
to yard and barn for
future use when winter
comes.
The sudden silence shocks:
the air suddenly without a sound.
In earlier days was little
sound
as horse drawn wagon crossed
the field where stooks had dried
then loaded with hay or
corn by two pronged ancient forks.
A few commands to patient horse
were all one heard
such is the change of course
with modern methods
mechanisation.

David Fairweather

Muskoka

Pampas, olive, forest green,
Sombre background, blood-red gashed,
Bank of orange, tangerine,
Red of rust, vermilion splashed;
Yellow ochre, yellow rose,
Golden, saffron, citron, sand,
Beaten copper, burnished bronze,
Bright brown calf-hide leather tanned.
Shot-silk colours, folkcloth weaves,
Phoenix feathers, flight of fire -
A hundred thousand flaming leaves
That burn skin to heart's desire.
The dull red glow of ember rake
Is mirrored in Muskoka Lake.

Catherine Gregory

Harvest Home

Children at the church door
Bearing gifts at harvest time
Readily to lay on the altar floor,
Ready to worship the Lord.
Here we have bread fresh and warm,
Fruits from the orchard trees,
Vegetables dug from the farm;
And tins bought from the shop.
Fresh spun wool off the old sheep,
Eggs small brown from the hen,
Babe in arms fast asleep
Heedless of the harvest hymns.
For now it is harvest home
And all is gathered in so safe
In barns built from warm red stone
Where wind cannot creep in.
Little harvest mouse in suit of grey,
Hurry scurry through the grain
For the winter time he may
Store well to endure.
Church door shut against the wind
That rustles though brown-gold leaves
Shaking the notices to the door pinned
As harvest is debated within.

J E Alban

God The Provider

God made the fish we take from the sea
And the ripened fruit we get off a tree
God made the cattle we kill for its meat
The birds and the sheep we all like to eat
God the provider who tends to our health
Provides in abundance with nature's wealth
God didn't allocate in climes which are poor
Endowed with poverty knocking at the door
God made the opulent gross and obese
Now he wants all Satan's gluttony to cease
God fed the multitude on fishes and bread
One of his great miracles so it is said
Then like the wheat that's threshed in the field
God wants us all to bear a fruitful yield

Francis Arthur Rawlinson

Harvest Home

At the sound of wild geese I pause to see
Hundreds like many a passing year
Taking me back to storks and elk and deer
And a life no longer lived by me.

My homeland hugs high sand dunes by the Baltic Sea
And rows of golden waving ears
Awaiting rich harvests amidst my tears
And a life no longer lived by me.

My homeland hugs high sand dunes by the Baltic Sea
And lingering memories of a happy home,
Fields, beaches, woods where I would roam
And a life no longer lived by me.

My homeland hugs high sand dunes by the Baltic Sea
Where huge clouds of glasnost begin to pour
Hope on its outcasts as never before
Of a life no longer lived by me.

Manfred Reuser

Granny Smith's? No - God's?

The stickers on my apples tell
Of exotic lands in which they fell.
The stalk sometimes a leaf may bear
As witness that a tree was there.
Shiny reds and greens all spotted,
Multi-coloured, mixtured, mottled.

Arranged in shops for all to view,
No effort is required of you,
The farmer toils in rain and sun -
And he is not the only one
Pickers and packers each globe prepare
Each one is precious, 'Handle with care'.

God watches each one grow from seed
The sun He sends or rain if need.
Pickers and packers, and farmers too,
He knows each one and what they do.
Each apple it is a work of love
To each of us, from God above.

Sue Falcon

Threshed

Breezes threshed no longer
to use our broken,
exhausted bodies:
So we can pray to God
forever more.
Harvest.

Kirk Antony Watson

The Gleaners

When I was young and the world was vast, it was such a joy to me
To meander through the cornfields or dream beneath a tree.
Whole families went out gleaning, from Baby Sue to Gran
And we settled by the hedgerow, where Mother used a fan
For the days were hot and sunny and flies were all about
As we munched potato pasties with no fear of growing stout.
Oh the nutty aroma of stubble as it prickled our bare, tender toes
And the squeal of delight as the brave harvest mouse used his
whiskers to tickle Dad's nose!
The sad scarlet poppies lay dying, destroyed by the big blue machine
Which flung large ears of corn by the wayside, the freshest we ever
had seen.
We gathered them all for our chickens who laid eggs for our
breakfast and tea.
Then we swam in the wide, murky river and tied an old rope to a
tree.
We took turns to swing over the water for the willow, though
slender, was strong.
But sometimes we'd suffer a 'bootie' which soon put an end to our
song!
We marvelled at hazelnuts peeping from their perfectly formed frilly
caps
But when eaten they tasted so bitter - not ready for burglars perhaps!
The heat of the sun on our bodies left us giddy as day turned to
night
As we trudged homeward bound quite exhausted, but happy, in
God's fading light.
Now adult I still stop and glory at the gifts we perceive fall around
And thank God for the beauty of Nature as the wonders of harvest
abound.

Eileen M Pratt

Lord Of All The Harvest

The Lord of all the harvest surveys His endless fields
The crop is ripe for gathering, the corn already white.
How may He get His harvest in when labourers are few
Without consigning treasure to the dark and stormy night?

One solitary reaper is all He has to send.
He trains Him well, instructs Him in the task that lies before.
With heavy heart, reluctantly, He sends Him out to work:
He loves His Son, the reaper, but He loves the harvest more.

The man takes on the burden, fully conscious of His role
Soon enlisting fellow workers: twelve new reapers set about
The crop, another seventy, but still they are too few.
The Lord's Son knows with sadness that His time is running out.

The harvesting soon claims His life, He dies with broken heart
But knows the treasured sheaves of wheat must still be gathered in.
There on the field, He makes His will and tells His men their due.
They, not fully comprehending, to complete the task begin.

He's left them gifts, available to all who join the work
And promises to send them help - an unseen mighty power
To finish the immeasurable task He faithfully began.
So, many more now join them in the lateness of the hour.

And still, the wayward corn triumphs, the job is not complete.
Daylight is now fading fast, the labourers asking all,
'Are there any other reapers who can lend a saving hand'
To gather in the precious sheaves? Have you not heard their call?

If so, what has been your reply, soon carried to the Lord?
'Not interested? No time to spare? Ask me another day?'
Forgetting you may need His help should famine come your way.
And when the Lord of all the harvest counts His crop, what will you say?

Glenys Godfrey

Heaven's Harvest!

Abundantly the Lord provides world grain for daily bread!
Enough in fact, to see that *every* nation is well fed.
Yet far across the seas, war and disease and famines rife!
Millions die from hunger, oh how *cheap* is *human life!*

If we loved God sincerely, we would *listen* to His plea,
'Go feed my flock and tend my lambs,
What you do for *them,* you do for *Me!'*
There *is* enough for each man's need
Grain supplies are kept in stores.
Yet bureaucracy and white men's greed,
Keep *locked* these storage doors!

Commendable maybe it *is,* each year at Harvest Time,
To furnish elderly and sick, with gifts, flowers, fruit and wine.
Yet, *more* blessed are the folk who cherish those without *a penny.*
They tread the path our *Lord* defined,
Who gave His *all,* - for *many!*

Marcia Elizabeth Jenkin